JACKIE ROBINSON

and the Breaking of the Color Barrier

by Russell Shorto

Gateway Civil Rights
The Millbrook Press
Brookfield, Connecticut

Photographs courtesy of: Eddie Keating: cover; National
Baseball Library, Cooperstown, New York: cover inset, 1,
2-3, 4, 7, 12 (all), 13 (all), 15, 16, 22, 23, 29, 30; The
Bettmann Archive: 8; Collector's Stadium: 9; Schomburg
Center for Research in Black Culture: 10, 18-19; AP/Wide
World Photos: 11, 21, 24, 26, 27; Baltimore Sun: 17.

Cataloging-in-Publication Data

Shorto, Russell
Jackie Robinson and the breaking of the color barrier.

32 p.; ill.: (Gateway Civil Rights)
Bibliography: p.
Includes index.

Summary: A biography of Jackie Robinson, the first
black player in major-league baseball.
1. Robinson, Jackie—1919-1972. 2. Black athletes.
3. Baseball.
B 1991
ISBN 1-878841-15-7

Thousands of spectators packed stadiums for Negro National League games.

In 1919, a boy named John Roosevelt Robinson was born on a farm in Georgia. His parents called him Jackie. His father was a sharecropper, a poor farmer who had to give most of his crop to the man who owned the land. When Jackie was just one year old, his father left the family and moved to Florida. Jackie's mother was left with five children to care for. She got her family on the train to Pasadena, California, where her brother lived. She hoped to find a better life there.

Jackie Robinson never forgave his father for leaving the family. He knew his father had had a hard life, but, he said, "he had no right to desert my mother and five children." As Jackie grew, he came to respect his mother for working so hard to support the family on her own. He always considered her the most important person in his life.

Jackie Robinson's uniform is on display at the Baseball Hall of Fame in Cooperstown, N.Y.

In Pasadena, Jackie's mother went to work cleaning other people's houses. Sometimes she worked at big dinner parties. Jackie and his brothers and sister liked that because they knew she would bring home leftover pieces of cake for them. Some days, this was the only food they got.

Life in California was hard for the Robinson family. They found that black people were not treated fairly in Pasadena, just as in the South. In the summertime, the Robinson children wanted to go to the public swimming pool, but blacks could only swim there one day a week. When they had a little money, Jackie and his brothers sometimes went to the movies, but they had to sit way in the back, in the ''blacks only'' area.

Many whites were prejudiced against blacks. That is, they felt that blacks were not as good as white people. Blacks were called names and treated poorly. But when Jackie Robinson entered school, he discovered that he was very good at something: sports. He played basketball, soccer, football—all sports. And he nearly always won. Soon, some of his classmates were sharing their lunches with him so that he would play on their team.

Jackie liked playing hard and winning. He found that white children respected him for this. He liked the feeling, which he had never experienced before. He made up his mind that he would always work hard to gain respect.

In high school, Jackie played every sport offered, including golf, tennis, and track and field. He was the star athlete of his school.

Jackie's older brother, Mack, was also a great athlete. In fact, Mack went to the 1936 Olympics in Berlin as a sprinter. Adolf Hitler, the German leader, was in the stands. Hitler hoped to prove to the world that his German athletes were the greatest. But Jesse Owens, the great black runner, won the gold medal, and Mack Robinson came in second. Back in Pasadena, the Robinson family celebrated Mack's success. Mack Robinson and Jesse Owens gave blacks all over the world something to be proud of.

Meanwhile, Jackie was playing sports for Pasadena Junior College. He broke the school record in the long jump, which had been set by none other than his brother Mack. The local newspapers took notice. Could it be that Jackie would become an even greater athlete than his brother?

Shortly afterward, Jackie received a scholarship to attend the University of California at Los Angeles. There, he met a bright and attractive student named Rachel Isum. He liked her very much, but Rachel thought he was too full of himself because he was the best athlete in the school. Still, Jackie decided he would try to win her over.

Jackie was a star on the UCLA track team.

In 1941, the United States entered World War II. Jackie Robinson was drafted into the army. He became a second lieutenant in an all-black battalion that was stationed at Camp Hood, Texas. While there, something happened that he would remember all his life. He got on a bus with a woman who was the wife of another officer. She was black, but very light skinned. The bus driver thought she was white. He did not like the idea of a black man sitting with a white woman.

''Get to the rear!'' he told Jackie.

At that time, blacks were forced to ride in the rear of buses in many cities. But such practices were not supposed to be legal on army posts. Jackie knew this, and he would not budge. The bus driver argued, and the military police soon showed up. Jackie was charged with being drunk, even though he had not drunk any alcohol. Newspapers covered the story. Eventually, Jackie was found not guilty. But Jackie Robinson was still angry. He had learned a bitter lesson. He later wrote, ''I was in two wars, one against the foreign enemy, the other against prejudice at home.''

Jackie suffered racial discrimination during his time in the U.S. Army.

Baseball

Jackie did not know what he would do for a career. He thought he might become a coach at a black college, but he was not sure. In 1944, he received an honorable discharge from the army. Soon after that, he joined the Kansas City Monarchs, a team in the Negro baseball leagues. The pay was $400 a month. Jackie was eager to make money so he could help support his mother.

During Jackie Robinson's childhood, major league baseball was very different from the way it is today. Baseball was segregated —only white men played in the major leagues. Blacks, Hispanics, and other minorities were not allowed to play. So black baseball players formed their own leagues. Many of the greatest players of all time were Negro league stars.

One of these Negro league stars was Satchel Paige. His real name was LeRoy, but he got the nickname Satchel as a boy because he used to earn money by helping people at the train station carry their satchels, or bags. Satchel was one of the all-time great pitchers. He was most famous for his fastball, which he liked to call his "bee ball." In 1948, after the color barrier was broken, Satchel joined the Cleveland Indians. By then, he had already pitched in the Negro leagues for 24 years.

Another of the all-time greats who played in the Negro leagues was Josh Gibson. Gibson played with the Pittsburgh Crawfords and other teams from 1933 to 1945. Many experts said he was a better hitter even than Babe Ruth. He once hit 89 home runs in a single season—29 more than Ruth's best. People said that he once hit a ball so far and so high that no one saw it come down. The umpire just shrugged and called it a home run. But despite Gibson's great talent, he earned only $6,000 in his best year, less than players in the all-white major leagues who were not nearly as talented.

This was still the situation in 1944, when Jackie Robinson joined the Kansas City Monarchs. Playing for the Monarchs was very hard work. Players in the Negro leagues had to put up with all the hardships that other blacks faced. When they came to new towns, they were not allowed to stay in most of the hotels. The players often wandered the streets for hours, looking for a place to sleep. Many restaurants would shut their doors on them. As Jackie later remembered, "You could never sit down to a relaxed hot meal."

Since money was tight, traveling was difficult. The players had to cram together in rickety buses, often driving for two days and nights, then playing a game as soon as they arrived in the new town.

Jackie was frustrated by this hard life. He did not think it was fair, and he did not want to continue playing in the Negro leagues. But he was determined to continue because he was trying to save up money to marry Rachel.

Things were soon to change, though. Jackie did not know it, but one of the most important men in baseball was trying to meet him. Branch Rickey, general manager of the Brooklyn Dodgers, was a man who had made many changes in professional baseball. Now he was about to make another.

Jackie played one season with the Kansas City Monarchs before signing with the Montreal Royals.

The Negro National League

Rube Foster

Rube Foster was a great pitcher in his day, but that was not all. He became the greatest manager in the history of black baseball. Rube played at the turn of the century, when black teams were not organized. There was a lot of enthusiasm, but not much money. There was a lot of skill, but not much training. Most important of all, there was no league. Rube Foster got to work to change all that.

In 1911, Rube started a team in Chicago called the American Giants. The Giants had a good field to play on, good equipment, and the best black players in the country. Rube Foster was their manager.

Rube was a hard man to work for. He told every player how to run, when to swing, and when to bunt. He believed in stealing bases, so all of his players became good base stealers. Their games were always exciting.

Rube trained his players well in the basics, and the American Giants won game after game. Encouraged by his success, Rube later decided to organize an entire black league. He called it the Negro National League. The first games were played in 1920.

Satchel Paige was one of the all-time great pitchers.

The Pittsburgh Crawfords, a Negro league team, in front of their team bus.

Posters advertised Negro league games.

The teams had fixed schedules, and players had regular salaries. The white newspapers never reported NNL games, but fans found out about them. Baseball fans loved the league because the games were so exciting and so well played. Sometimes, crowds of over 10,000 people attended NNL games.

Over the years, several other black leagues were formed. Conditions were hard, because black ballplayers still faced racial prejudice in every town they traveled to. But they were professionals playing in an organized system, just like the all-white major leagues.

Rube Foster died in 1930, but the Negro leagues lived on, exhibiting some of the nation's greatest talent. In 1947, when Jackie Robinson joined the major leagues, the Negro leagues began to die out. As more black players were signed to major league contracts, the black teams lost their best talent. The great teams became only a memory.

Josh Gibson was one of the best hitters in history.

"Can You Do It?"

Branch Rickey was famous in baseball circles. When he made a move, everyone took notice. In 1943, rumors spread that Rickey was going to start a Negro team called the Brown Dodgers. Rickey sent his scouts out to look at promising young blacks. These scouts were personally opposed to blacks playing major league baseball, but they were willing to help Rickey look for players for a new team in the Negro leagues.

The scouts thought what they wanted, but Branch Rickey had another idea. He had no intention of starting a black team. Instead, he was about to shock the baseball world by signing the first black player to a major league contract. He had wanted to do this years before, while he was the general manager of the St. Louis Cardinals, but it was impossible then. Segregation was so strong in St. Louis that blacks who went to major league baseball games had to sit in a separate section. The idea of blacks playing in the games was unthinkable.

But now that Rickey was in Brooklyn, things were different. He sent word to Jackie Robinson that he wanted to meet with him. Jackie agreed, and in August 1945 he traveled to New York, thinking that Rickey wanted him to play for a black team. But Jackie soon learned the truth. Rickey shook hands with Jackie but then began taunting him, calling him a nigger. Jackie was confused.

Branch Rickey

"Mr. Baseball"—that was one of Branch Rickey's nicknames. He was one of the most important people in the history of the game. He invented the farm club system, which allowed young players to gain experience playing organized baseball in the minor leagues.

But Branch Rickey's biggest contribution was to help Jackie Robinson break the color barrier. This had been a dream of Rickey's for many years. In 1910, he was the coach of a college team in Ohio. One day, the team traveled to South Bend, Indiana, for a game. The whites on the team checked into a hotel, but the manager of the hotel would not let the team's one black player check in. He said the hotel did not accept blacks. Finally, Branch Rickey got the manager to let the player stay with Rickey on a cot in his room. Later that night, the player sat up crying because he felt so ashamed and hurt. Branch Rickey never forgot that painful scene.

He got his chance to change things in 1945, when he signed Jackie Robinson. Many old-timers were furious. Once, after he gave a speech about integration, a man came up to him and tried to wrestle him to the ground. But these incidents soon stopped. Over the next few years, every pro team signed black players. An important step in the civil rights movement had been taken.

"Can you take that?" Rickey asked. He wanted Jackie to under-stand that as the first black player in the major leagues, he would get a lot of racial abuse. He wanted to make sure Jackie would "turn the other cheek" and ignore the abuse, rather than try to fight back. If Jackie argued, he could ruin the chances of other black players who might follow him. It would be better to show America that he was above name-calling. He had to impress the nation with his baseball skills, not his fighting skills.

Jackie was not sure he liked this. He asked if Rickey was looking for a black player who was afraid to fight back.

Branch Rickey's eyes lit up. "I'm looking for a ballplayer with guts enough not to fight back!" he cried. "Can you do it?"

Jackie thought for a while. Then he said, "I think I can." "Thinking isn't enough," Rickey told him. "Can you?"

Jackie at his major league tryout.

Brooklyn Signs Negro Player, First In Organized Baseball

Montreal, Oct. 23 (AP)—The first Negro player ever to be admitted to organized baseball was signed tonight by the Brooklyn Dodgers for their International League farm club, the Montreal Royals.

Jackie Robinson, one-time U.C.L.A. halfback ace and recent shortstop of the Kansas City Negro Monarchs, put his signature on a contract calling not only for a regular player's salary, but also for a

Jackie made up his mind. He had learned a lot from his mother. One of her lessons was that it is often wiser to turn the other cheek than to fight back. "I can," Jackie said.

That year, Jackie and Rachel were finally married. Soon afterward, Jackie appeared at the training camp of the Montreal Royals, one of the Dodgers' farm clubs. A farm club is a team in the minor leagues in which promising players show whether or not they have enough talent to play in the majors.

Jackie would have to prove himself in Montreal. Some fans there were angry, but others were curious to see how well a black would play in the minors. They soon got their answer.

The first game of the Royals' 1946 season was played in Jersey City, New Jersey. The stadium was packed with a sellout crowd of 52,000. People were happy because World War II was over and because the start of a new baseball season is always a time of celebration. Everyone was also eager to see the league's first black player. As the national anthem played, Jackie Robinson felt a lump in his throat and a nervous quiver in his stomach. He knew everyone was there to see him.

Stealing bases was one of Jackie's specialties—both in Montreal and in Brooklyn.

Jackie was the second batter. The first batter grounded out. Then Jackie walked to the plate in a funny pigeon-toed way that would soon become famous. He was stocky and thickly muscled. He watched a fastball zip past and did not swing. Then a second flew across the plate. Finally, on the third pitch, he swung the bat. The ball bounced to the shortstop, who threw to first base. Jackie Robinson was out.

People in the stands looked at one another. They had heard that Robinson was a great hitter. But it did not take a great hitter to ground out. Some wondered whether he would make it to the big leagues.

Jackie came up to bat again in the third inning. Now there were two men on base and no outs. The other team had heard that Jackie was a great bunter. They thought he would try to bunt, so the infield moved in close. The pitcher wound up and threw a hard fastball.

Crack! The ball sailed in a high arc over the left field fence. Jackie Robinson had hit a home run! Three runs were scored on the hit, and the crowd erupted into cheers. Jackie got three more hits in the game and stole two bases. The Royals went on to win, 14 to 1. Newspapers reported that Jackie Robinson had stolen the show and had proved that blacks deserved a place in major league baseball.

It was a great year. Jackie Robinson led his team to the International League championship and finished his first season as the league's batting champ. He also led the league in runs scored.

Black America was proud. A few years earlier, Joe Louis, the boxing champ, had been the hero of young blacks around the

Jackie Robinson with Dodger teammate Peewee Reese.

nation. Now they also cheered on Jackie Robinson, the hero of the minor leagues.

The Major Leagues

The next year, the Royals wanted Jackie back, but Branch Rickey had other plans. It was time to call Jackie up to the major leagues. Rickey was not doing this simply to help the civil rights movement. The fact was, the Brooklyn Dodgers were in trouble. They needed new players if they were to start winning. Branch Rickey always said that his first goal was to win championships and that he would sign any player—black, white, or purple—who would help his team win. Rickey now believed that Jackie Robinson was such a man.

Jackie played his first game in the major leagues on April 15, 1947. Ebbets Field, the Dodgers' home stadium, was filled to overflowing. Everyone wanted to see Robinson, Number 42, work miracles.

They were disappointed. Jackie was nervous and went into a batting slump. He did not get a hit that game or in the next several. The pressure was intense for the league's first black player, and Jackie had a hard time dealing with it. Fans yelled insults. Pitchers threw bean balls at him, which meant that they aimed for his head. Jackie and Rachel now had a baby boy, and they got letters at home from people who threatened to kidnap the child if Jackie did not quit.

One day the Dodgers came to Philadelphia for a game against the Phillies. The Philadelphia players hurled insults at Jackie. "Hey, nigger, why don't you go back to the cotton field where you belong?" "They're waiting for you in the jungle, black boy!"

Jackie later said this was the worst day of his life. He was breaking the color barrier all alone, and he felt very sad and lonely.

But he hung in there. Soon he came out of his slump and started to hit the ball. He finished the season batting .297, led the Dodgers in home runs, and led the league in stolen bases. He was named National League Rookie of the Year. Players on other teams stopped calling him names. One manager told his players, "Don't get him madder than he is."

That first season ended a success, but it was hard on Jackie. Many of his own teammates were against the idea of playing with a black. In fact, many had never talked with a black man in their lives. They had strange ideas about black people. The team's manager, Burt Shotton, later said, "At the time Jackie joined the Dodgers, I am sure that I wouldn't have invited him to sit with me in the dining car." But things changed as Jackie spent time with the team and the others got to know him. Burt Shotton said it was "merely a matter of education." So the players learned, but many fans still taunted Jackie.

Jackie's cap is now in the Baseball Hall of Fame.

Once he got a letter saying he would be shot if he played a game in Cincinnati. The other players were concerned, and one suggested that they all wear Jackie's number.

But the fans' prejudice passed also. Change came quickly. Once Jackie Robinson broke the color barrier, other teams recruited talented black players. Larry Doby, the great Negro league slugger, signed with the Cleveland Indians in 1948 and broke the color barrier in the American League. That same year, Branch Rickey signed another star of the Negro leagues, Roy Campanella. Campanella was destined to become the greatest catcher in Dodger history.

The cover of the program to the 1947 World Series between the Brooklyn Dodgers and the New York Yankees.

Two years after Jackie played his first game as a Dodger, nearly every major league team had at least one black player. By that time, most fans had come to judge players by their ability and not by their skin color.

Meanwhile, Jackie Robinson got better and better. He won the National League batting championship in 1949 and was voted the league's Most Valuable Player the same year. For 10 years, he played as a Brooklyn Dodger. He led the team to the World Series six times.

Jackie steals home against the Boston Braves.

In six straight years, he batted at least .300. He also won a reputation as a fearsome baserunner. He terrorized pitchers with his daring leads and twice led the National League in stolen bases.

But Jackie Robinson was more than a great baseball player. He was the man who broke the color barrier. After living under racial prejudice his whole life, Jackie had helped improve conditions for blacks in baseball. After this, he became dedicated to helping blacks in other ways. He became active in politics.

In 1949, Jackie disagreed with statements made by the famous black singer, Paul Robeson. Robeson declared that if the United States got into a war with the Soviet Union, blacks should not fight because blacks were not treated fairly in the United States. Jackie Robinson, as a leader in the black community, was asked for his opinion.

Jackie was angry. He said that he could not speak for others, but that he believed in standing up for his country. He knew that racial prejudice was a major problem in the United States, but he believed that in the United States, he and other blacks could work to change things.

After this, Jackie became known as a black spokesman.

As his career went on, Jackie's popularity grew. In 1950, his salary was $35,000, the most any Dodger had ever received. A year later, a movie about his life was released, *The Jackie Robinson Story*.

In 1956, Jackie knew that his career was winding down. He decided he would retire at the end of the year. The Dodgers' president, Walter O'Malley, surprised him, however, by telling him that he had been traded to the New York Giants. Jackie, in turn, came out with his own surprise. He announced his retirement.

The next year, the Dodgers moved to Los Angeles. Suddenly the Dodgers were gone from Brooklyn, and Jackie Robinson was gone from baseball. To many fans, it was the end of an era.

Life After Baseball

Following his baseball career, Jackie Robinson devoted time to his family. He and Rachel now had two sons, David and Jackie, Jr., and a daughter, Sharon. Jackie also gave political speeches. He admired Martin Luther King, Jr., the leader of the civil rights movement. But King favored nonviolent struggle to achieve black equality. Jackie did not always agree with this. He had a fiery streak. Another great leader of the civil rights movement was Malcolm X, who favored strong, sometimes violent action. Jackie disagreed with Malcolm X's position also. His own views were in between those of the two great civil rights leaders.

Jackie Robinson took part in many protests to end racial discrimination.

People like Martin Luther King, Jr., and Malcolm X led the civil rights struggle in the 1960s. But Jackie Robinson had made a big contribution back in 1947, when he put on a Brooklyn Dodgers uniform. When fans saw blacks and whites playing together, some realized that blacks and whites could also live together as equals.

In 1962, Jackie Robinson was named to baseball's Hall of Fame. As his plaque was unveiled, three people stood beside him. One was his mother, who had raised him through the hard times. The second was his wife, Rachel. And the third was an ailing 80-year-old white man, Branch Rickey.

Three years later, in 1965, Rickey died. Jackie always re-

Jackie received an honorary degree from Howard University in Washington, D.C. Martin Luther King, Jr., was also honored.

membered how Rickey had believed in him. After Rickey's death, Jackie said the old man had been like a father to him.

For the next several years, Jackie continued to fight for black rights. He also fought an illness, which became worse every year.

Finally, in 1972, Jackie Robinson died at the young age of 53. Thousands of people attended his funeral.

By the time of Jackie Robinson's death, professional sports had changed a great deal. Blacks played in pro baseball, pro football and pro basketball. Even today, however, blacks in pro sports are not completely equal. There are very few black managers and coaches, and there is still a way to go to achieve equality. Every year, a small step is made. But the biggest step was the first one, the one that broke the color barrier. And it was taken by a stocky, pigeon-toed man from Georgia.

Important Dates in the Life of Jackie Robinson

1919 Jackie is born on January 31, in Cairo, Georgia.

1936 Jackie's brother Mack wins a silver medal at the Berlin Olympics.

1942 Jackie enters the U.S. Army.

1944 Jackie leaves the army; he joins the Kansas City Monarchs of the Negro National League.

1945 Jackie marries Rachel Isum. Jackie meets Branch Rickey; he is signed to a Brooklyn Dodger farm club.

1947 Jackie breaks the color barrier in major league baseball on April 15, at Ebbets Field, Brooklyn.

1949 Jackie wins the National League's batting championship; he is voted the league's Most Valuable Player.

1957 Jackie retires from baseball.

1962 Jackie is named to the baseball Hall of Fame.

1972 Jackie Robinson dies in Stamford, Connecticut, on October 24.

JACK ROOSEVELT ROBINSON

BROOKLYN N.L. 1947 TO 1956
LEADING N.L. BATTER IN 1949. HOLDS
FIELDING MARK FOR SECOND BASEMAN
PLAYING IN 150 OR MORE GAMES WITH .992.
LED N.L. IN STOLEN BASES IN 1947 AND
1949. MOST VALUABLE PLAYER IN 1949.
LIFETIME BATTING AVERAGE .311. JOINT
RECORD HOLDER FOR MOST DOUBLE PLAYS
BY SECOND BASEMAN, 137 IN 1951.
LED SECOND BASEMEN IN DOUBLE
PLAYS 1949-50-51-52.

Find Out More About Jackie Robinson

Books: *Jackie Robinson: He Was the First* by David A. Adler (New York: Holiday House, 1989).

Paul Robeson: Citizen of the World by Shirley Graham (New York: Simon & Schuster, 1971).

Mr. Baseball: The Story of Branch Rickey by David Lipman (New York: Putnam's, 1966).

Films: *The Jackie Robinson Story* (1950) is about Jackie's breaking of the color barrier, and it features Jackie playing himself.

The Bingo Long Traveling All-Stars and Motor Kings (1976) is a comedy about the Negro National League. It stars Billy Dee Williams, James Earl Jones, and Richard Pryor.

Places: The Baseball Hall of Fame is located in Cooperstown, New York. It has an exhibit on black baseball and the Negro National League. It also has Jackie Robinson's Dodger baseball cap and uniform on display.

Jackie Robinson's Hall of Fame plaque.

Index